# 30-MINUTE GROUPS

# ONLINE SAFETY

## FOR MIDDLE AND HIGH SCHOOL

*SPOTTING RED FLAGS, PROTECTING PRIVACY, AND BEING A POSITIVE VOICE*

DR. RAYCHELLE CASSADA LOHMANN

NATIONAL CENTER for
**YOUTH ISSUES**

# Duplication and Copyright

No part of this publication may be reproduced, stored in a retrieval system, or transmitted in any form by any means, electronic, mechanical, photocopy, video or audio recording, or otherwise without prior written permission from the publisher, except for all worksheets and activities which may be reproduced for a specific group or class. Reproduction for an entire school or school district is prohibited.

NATIONAL CENTER for
**YOUTH ISSUES**

P.O. Box 22185
Chattanooga, TN 37422-2185
423.899.5714 • 866.318.6294
fax: 423.899.4547 • www.ncyi.org

ISBN: 9781965066041

© 2025 National Center for Youth Issues, Chattanooga, TN

All rights reserved.

Written by: Raychelle Cassada Lohmann, Ph. D.

Published by National Center for Youth Issues

Printed in the U.S.A. • January 2025

Third party links are accurate at the time of publication, but may change over time.

The information in this book is designed to provide helpful information on the subjects discussed and is not intended to be used, nor should it be used, to diagnose or treat any mental health or medical condition. For diagnosis or treatment of any mental health or medical issue, consult a licensed counselor, psychologist, or physician. The publisher and author are not responsible for any specific mental or physical health needs that may require medical supervision, and are not liable for any damages or negative consequences from any treatment, action, application, or preparation, to any person reading or following the information in this book. References are provided for informational purposes only and do not constitute endorsement of any websites or other sources.

ASCA National Model®, Recognized ASCA Model Program® and RAMP® are registered trademarks of the American School Counselor Association. Our use of them does not imply an affiliation with or endorsement by the American School Counselor Association.

# Contents

# Introduction

*Online Safety for Middle and High School* is designed to help you teach students the importance of online safety. It encourages members to engage in open dialogues, explore ethical situations, and, more importantly, apply what they learn during their screen time. To provide a robust lesson and group experience, use this book alongside the *15-Minute Focus Digital Citizenship: Supporting Youth Navigating Technology in a Rapidly Changing World*.[1] Both books offer abundant lessons, information, and tools to help you instill the message of online safety, digital literacy, and digital citizenship.

As you work through this workbook, you'll notice it has ten sessions broken into four sections. The materials are formatted so you can pull a single activity or focus on specific questions to work through with participants. The book provides flexibility for using the resources you'd like while ensuring sufficient content to cover a full lesson. Below is an explanation of what's included in each chapter so that you can design a robust experiential learning experience for your students.

I sincerely hope you enjoy the flexible nature of this book as you guide your students to practice safe behaviors when they are on their devices. Your role is invaluable in assisting students to become upstanding digital citizens and learn how to live safely in a digital world. *Thank you for all you do to prepare the next generation of digital citizens!*

## See page 75 for information on Downloadable Resources.

## What's Included?

**Online Safety** offers a comprehensive ten-lesson program and accompanying materials for facilitating group sessions. Following each detailed lesson outline, you'll find practical resources for establishing a small group within your school environment.

**Mind Map:** Provides an illustrated diagram of technological terms that foster critical skills that help students navigate the digital world responsibly. Terms are located at the beginning of each lesson. Emphasize how each word connects to making informed choices, protecting personal information, and interacting respectfully online. Students should begin each lesson by considering the meaning of the specific term or concept. Mind maps are optional, but visuals are helpful for many students. Some have found it helpful to draw the Mind Map on the board.

**ASCA® Standards** are incorporated into every lesson to ensure alignment with educational goals.

**Lesson Introductions** provide clear explanations of key concepts to set the stage for each lesson.

**Lesson Objectives** present structure and direction to help students understand what they are learning and why the content is essential in their lives.

**Key Terms** assist the facilitator with common terms used throughout the chapter.

**Icebreakers** offer a structured approach to initiating group discussions. These prompts encourage student engagement, sharing, and deeper topic comprehension.

**Activities** enhance learning by engaging in experiential exercises that encourage outside-of-the-box thinking and application to real-world problems.

**Quizzes and Worksheets** engage students in brain-boosting activities to stimulate the brain and help them grasp key concepts.

**Discussion Questions** spark critical thinking and reflection on the lesson content.

**Skill Builder** activities, including round-robin discussions, offer opportunities for students to apply newly acquired skills in a supportive group setting.

**What Would You Do?** Engage students in answering hypothetical questions that prompt analytical and critical thinking skills and promote ethical decision-making and problem-solving abilities.

**Closing Considerations** summarize key points and invite students to reflect on their learning journey as they learn new concepts and strategies.

## Accompanying Group Documents

The **Small Group Action Plan Guide** provides instructions for implementing the ASCA® National Model within a small-group setting.

A **Permission Form** is included to obtain parental consent for student participation in the group. For the best response, send these home two weeks before a new small group starts.

**Group Expectations** outline behavioral guidelines for group members and provide space for customization.

The **Group Attendance Form** is a tool for tracking student attendance and session topics.

The **Group Attendance Form (Example)** demonstrates effective use of the attendance form.

**Pre- and Post-Group Surveys** assess students' knowledge and understanding of the program's concepts. To measure student growth, administer the pre-group survey before instruction, followed by the post-group survey upon completion. Calculate the percentage of improvement by comparing pre-and post-survey averages.

### Percentage of Improvement Formula:
(Post-Group Total - Pre-Group Total / Pre-Group Total) x 100 = Percentage of Overall Improvement

### Example:
(30 Post-Group Total - 19 Pre-Group Total / 19) x 100 = 57.89% Overall Improvement

Analyze student data, including conduct referrals, attendance, and academic performance, to identify potential group participants. Monitor student progress closely and share results with your advisory council.

The **Post-Group Survey Results** template demonstrates how to visually represent data for stakeholders. Utilize graphs and charts to communicate findings effectively.

A **Certificate of Completion** recognizes students' achievements upon finishing the small group.

**Online Safety Group Completion Letters** provide parents/guardians with curriculum highlights and student progress.

**Additional Materials:** This small group workbook includes all essential components, though you will need to make copies of some activities and prepare group discussion materials. Having art supplies and fidgets available can enhance the group experience.

*Wishing you much success with your group! May your students gain a lot from this valuable learning experience!*

# Introductory Group Session

## Directions & Overview

Conduct this introductory session before starting the regular lessons. This initial meeting will acclimate students to the program's structure, expectations, and foundational tools.

**Directions:** Begin by extending a warm welcome to all participants. Communicate the group's objectives and generate enthusiasm for learning and collaboration.

**Survey:** Before proceeding, read the pre-group survey instructions aloud to the students and have each student complete the form. Carefully examine the completed forms to verify that all questions have been answered.

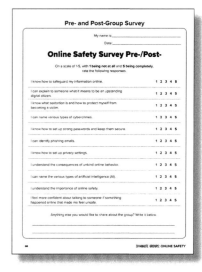

**Introductions:** Foster a sense of community by encouraging students to share their names, something about themselves, and what they wish to learn in the group.

**Explain the Group Format:** Explain where and how often you will meet. Share the list of topics. Explain that, in each meeting, you will discuss one of the topics together, then talk through various scenarios, complete individual and group activities, and answer questions.

**Review Group Expectations:** Print a copy of the Group Expectations. Review the expectations together with the students and answer questions as they arise. Collaborate with your group to determine whether you need to modify or add expectations.

**Group Conclusion:** Ask each student to summarize the information they learned from this session into one sentence. Students may share with their partners or the group.

**Note to Facilitators:** You can customize the material to fit the needs of your group. If you're working with reticent students, they can write their responses to questions instead of sharing them aloud or break into smaller teams to discuss. Some facilitators may incorporate traditional games into the lessons if they have longer session times. Remember, the workbook is just the framework, but you will bring it to life!

# TECHNOLOGY AWARENESS AND USE

# Technology Use

## MIND MAP

On the board, draw a mind map and ask students to consider how they use *technology*.

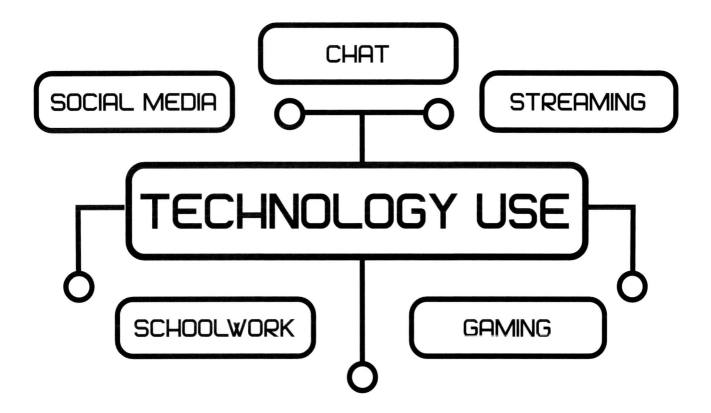

## ASCA® STANDARDS

- **B-SMS 1.** Responsibility for self and actions

- **B-SMS 2.** Self-discipline and self-control

- **B-SMS 8.** Balance of school, home, and community activities

## DIRECTIONS

Review the Group Expectations before reviewing the Mind Map. Then, read the Lesson Introduction and talk through the Key Terms for the lesson. Ask the Ice Breaker Questions and complete the Activity. Students can then work in pairs to craft their responses to the Discussion Questions or share with the whole group. Complete the Skill Builder and What Would You Do? game, as time allows. Be sure to complete the Closing Considerations with each lesson.

## LESSON INTRODUCTION

Most people, including young people, spend half their daily waking hours online. A Gallup survey found that over half of U.S. teens spend nearly 4.8 hours each day on social media, more than many spend daily on schoolwork.[2] Now, that's a lot of screen time. In this session, you'll ask participants to become aware of their technology usage and how it impacts their lives positively and negatively. You'll also begin laying the foundation of online safety and instilling the importance of disconnecting from technology and connecting with life.

## LESSON OBJECTIVES

During this session, participants will:

1. Assess their device usage and increase self-awareness of online time.

2. Examine the impacts of excessive screen time on productivity, relationships, and overall well-being.

3. Identify challenges from excessive device use, such as difficulties completing tasks or conflicts with peers or family members.

4. Learn strategies to manage screen time effectively, ensuring it does not interfere with other responsibilities or social interactions.

## KEY TERMS

Below are some common terms used throughout this chapter.

- **Internet Addiction,** also known as **Problematic Internet Use** (PIU), is the excessive use of the Internet that leads to adverse outcomes.

- **Online Identity**, also known as an internet persona, is the digital information we share and leave behind online. This digital information is also known as our "online footprint."

- **Nomophobia** is a fear of being without a cellular device or the internet.

Engage students in the following discussion. Ask them follow-up questions to expand on answers and encourage participation.

- What was your first electronic device?
- How old were you when you got this device? If it wasn't a phone, ask how old they were when they got their first phone.
- How strict are your parents concerning screen time?
- Do you set your own rules regarding screen time?
- What are some of the positives of having and using technology?
- What are some of the negatives of having and using technology?
- How much time do you spend online a day?

## ACTIVITY

# How is Your Technology Use Affecting You? Quiz

Did you know most devices track how much time you spend on them? Your screen settings allow you to compare your daily usage throughout the week to pinpoint the days and times you are most often online. Many apps will even break down your usage further by giving you specific information about how frequently you use them. There are even apps designed to help you monitor your online activities. Too much screen time can hurt your well-being and even create an addictive disorder known as "Internet Addiction" or *nomophobia* (fear of being without a mobile phone). Let's take the **How if Your Technology Use Affecting You? Quiz** to explore how much time you spend on your device and explore ways to create a healthy balance between school and home.

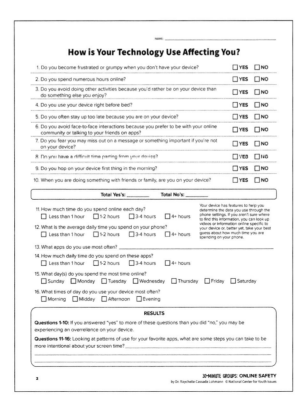

1. Do you become frustrated or grumpy when you don't have your device?

2. Do you spend numerous hours online?

3. Do you avoid doing other activities because you'd rather be on your device than do something else you enjoy?

4. Do you use your device right before bed?

5. Do you often stay up too late because you are on your device?

6. Do you avoid face-to-face interactions because you prefer to be with your online community or talking to your friends on apps?

7. Do you fear you may miss out on a message or something important if you're not on your device?

8. Do you have a difficult time parting from your device?

9. Do you hop on your device first thing in the morning?

10. When you are doing something with friends or family, are you on your device?

11. How much time do you spend online?

12. What is the average daily time you spend on your phone?

13. What apps do you use most often?

14. How much daily time do you spend on these apps?

15. What day(s) do you spend the most time online?

16. What times of day do you use your device most often?

**RESULTS:**

Questions 1-10: If you answered "yes" to more of these questions than you did "no," you may be experiencing an overreliance on your device.

Questions 11-16: Looking at patterns of use for your favorite apps, what are some steps you can take to be more intentional about your screen time?

After students have completed the worksheet, ask them to answer the following questions:

- How much time do you spend daily on your device?

- Does the amount of time you spend match up to the research, 40 hours a week?

- Do you notice any patterns in your online use? For example, are you on your device before school, and does it cause you to be late to class? Are you on your device late at night most nights of the week?

- What else would you be doing if you weren't online?

- What are some ways that you can better monitor and balance your screen time? For example, you could set up your device with time constraints or shut it down after a certain time.

Look for similarities and themes and bring those up during their discussions.

# Shut-It-Down Challenge

Now, let's take it to the next level. I'd like to offer up a challenge. We'll call it the Shut-It-Down Challenge, and here is how it will work: Shut down all electronic devices for 90 minutes each day. You may even need to remove the devices from your sight so you are not tempted to check them. During this time, choose one or two activities you like or would like to learn to do. You can choose to do something different every day.

Examples may include:

- Baking cookies or cupcakes
- Building something
- Cooking dinner
- Crocheting
- Dancing
- Drawing
- Exercising
- Painting
- Going for a walk with a friend

Have students share what activity they'll engage in during their device "Shut Down." Tell them to keep track of what they did during their 90 minutes of daily disconnection and plan to share during the next session.

## WHAT WOULD YOU DO?

Work through the following dilemma with students.

*Lauren's friend Kara needed to use Lauren's phone to text her mom to say that she was spending time together after school and would need a ride home. Kara asked to use Lauren's phone, so Lauren handed it over. Kara realized Lauren's phone was passcode protected and asked her for the code. Without thinking, Lauren told her the code. While on the phone, Kara started reading Lauren's texts and even replied under the guise of Lauren. When Lauren found out, she was beyond angry!*

Discussion Questions:

- How should Lauren handle this situation?
- What steps could Lauren have taken to protect her information better?

## CLOSING CONSIDERATIONS

Today, we discussed how much time we spend on our devices and the pros and cons of technology. You even pinpointed when you spent too much time online and identified things you could do without using your device. Over the next week, you agreed to set aside 90 minutes daily to disconnect and power off your device. Pay close attention to how you feel and what you do during that device-free time.

# CHAPTER 2

# Social Media: Pros and Cons

## MIND MAP

On the board, draw a mind map and ask students to consider the *pros and cons of technology*.

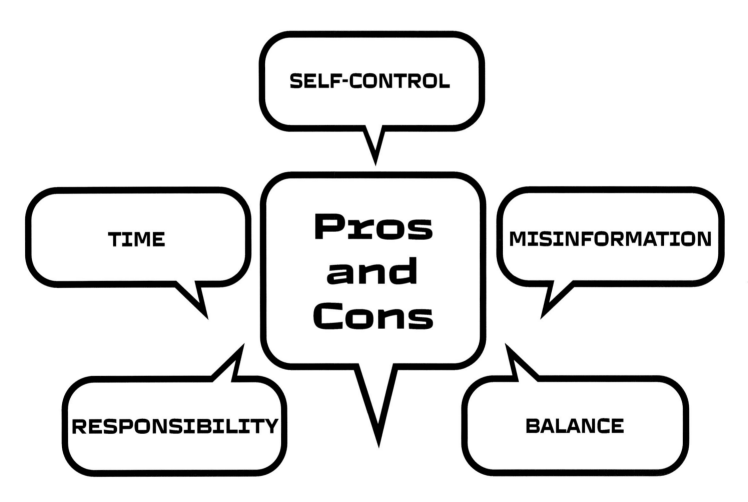

## ASCA® STANDARDS

- **B-SMS 2.** Self-discipline and self-control
- **B-SMS 8.** Balance of school, home, and community activities
- **B-SS 5.** Ethical decision-making and social responsibility

## DIRECTIONS

Review the Group Expectations before reviewing the Mind Map. Then, read the Lesson Introduction and talk through the Key Terms for the lesson. Ask the Ice Breaker Questions and complete the Activity. Students can then work in pairs to craft their responses to the Discussion Questions or share with the whole group. Complete the Skill Builder and What Would You Do? game, as time allows. Be sure to complete the Closing Considerations with each lesson.

## LESSON INTRODUCTION

Take a moment to have students share how their Shut-It-Down Challenge went and what activities they engaged in while their devices were off. Also, ask students what they learned from this challenge that they will carry with them.

Today, we will explore social media's pros and cons. Social media can be traced back to the 1980s. Since then, it has exploded into revolutionary ways for us to share ideas, thoughts, and information through virtual communities. It's also a great way to stay connected to family and friends who live abroad. On the other hand, social media can consume a lot of time, cause loss of time, create isolation, and lead to misinformation and miscommunication. Today, we'll dive deeper into what social media apps you use and the pros and cons of social media in your life.

## LESSON OBJECTIVES

During this session, participants will:

1. Learn to navigate virtual spaces securely.

2. Identify social media platform usage and the purposes behind its use.

3. Examine the negative consequences of overreliance on social media, including time management issues, potential for addiction, and impacts on mental health.

4. Learn strategies for maintaining a healthy approach to social media usage, emphasizing responsible and mindful engagement.

## KEY TERMS

Below are some common terms used throughout this chapter.

- **Digital Citizenship** is the sum of our online behaviors and decisions that impact self, others, and community.

- **Online Identity**, also known as internet persona, is the sum of information we share and leave behind when we are online.

- **Social Media** is a means for people to connect and share information online.

Use the round-robin method to engage students in answering the following questions. Encourage engagement by having them elaborate on their responses.

**Would You Rather?**

- Travel all 50 U.S. states or visit 5 different countries?

- Make a lot of money doing a job you dislike or earn less doing something you love?

- Have a large group of casual friends or a few really close, supportive friends?

- Be famous for something trivial (like a viral video) or known for making a positive difference in your community?

- Always have to tell the truth or never be able to speak at all?

- Have the ability to fly or be invisible?

## ACTIVITY

# Social Media Apps

NAME: _____

**Social Media Apps**

1. What social media apps do you frequently use?

| Social Media Apps | # of Friends/Followers |
| --- | --- |
| | |
| | |
| | |
| | |
| | |
| | |

2. What are the pros of social media?

3. Share something positive that has happened on a social media site.

4. What are the cons of social media?

5. Share an instance where something negative occurred on a social media site.

6. What do the words "online identity" mean to you?

7. What does it mean to be a good digital citizen?

30-MINUTE GROUPS: ONLINE SAFETY
by Dr. Raychelle Cassada Lohmann © National Center for Youth Issues

Using the **Social Media Apps Worksheet**, guide the students through the worksheet by asking the questions below.

1. **What social media apps do you frequently use?**

   - Write them down.

   - How many followers or friends do you have on your social media apps? Look at your number of friends and/or followers and write down how many beside each app you listed.

   - Do you know all your friends and/or followers personally? (Meaning you've met them in person.)

   - If you had to delete two apps from your device right now what would you delete? Draw an **X** through these apps on your list. Why did you choose those apps?

   - Which two apps would you keep? Draw an asterisk * next to these apps. Why did you choose those apps?

2. **What are the pros of social media?**

3. **Share something positive that has happened on a social media site.**
   This experience may have happened to you, or you may have witnessed it happening to another person. It may even be a story read about something that happened to someone on social media.

4. **What are the cons of social media?**

5. **Share an instance where something negative occurred on a social media site.**
   This experience may have happened to you, or you may have witnessed it happening to another person. It may even be a story read about something that happened to someone on social media.

6. **What do the words "online identity" mean to you?**

7. **What does it mean to be a good digital citizen?**

**Alternate Method:**

There are excellent tools available that allow students to type their responses on their phones, which then form a word cloud displayed on a screen. This method ensures anonymity and helps them feel more connected as they see similar responses from their peers.

## SKILL BUILDER

# Two-Sided Coin

Social media use is like a two-sided coin; there are two different ways of viewing things. Social media has both positive and negative aspects. Earlier, we discussed some pros and cons of social media use, but now we are going to take a deeper dive into exploring the advantages and disadvantages. Now, let's break into two teams:

- Team 1 – Pro Team will focus on the positive side (heads) of social media use.

- Team 2 – Con Team will focus on social media use's negative side (tails).

Allow each team at least 10 minutes to brainstorm as many aspects of their assigned stance as possible. pros and cons as possible. Then, have them choose their top three points to debate with the opposing team. Once time has passed, flip a coin to see which team begins the debate. Teams should assign roles such as the topic presenter (opening speaker), rebuttal speakers (there can be more than one, and they will need to take turns), and the closing speaker. The facilitator will act as a moderator and timekeeper to ensure each side gets an opportunity to state their point.

Following the debate, the teams unite and reflect on what they gained from the discussion and how social media is a two-sided coin.

## WHAT WOULD YOU DO?

Work through the following dilemma with students.

*Connor had a difficult breakup and needed a friend to talk to. So, he went over to his friend Jacob's house. When he arrived, Jacob was in his room watching funny videos on his phone. Jacob invited him in and started sharing his phone screen with Connor. Unfortunately, Connor's mind was elsewhere, and he wasn't in the mood for funny clips. Whenever Connor tried to talk to his friend, Jacob would laugh, saying, "You've got to see this..." Connor felt like Jacob wasn't hearing a word he was saying. To Connor, it felt like Jacob's phone was way more important than his friend. Connor got up to leave, and Jacob looked up and asked Connor, "Hey, where are you going?" Connor just kept on walking.*

Discussion Questions:

- What would you do if you were in Connor's situation?
- Have you ever been in a situation where someone was more interested in their screen than listening or paying attention to you?
- How did it make you feel?
- Have you ever been in a situation where you were the one not paying attention? What happened?

## CLOSING CONSIDERATIONS

Today, we discussed the pros and cons of social media and identified how much we use it in our daily lives. We worked through a situation where our devices kept us from being present with a friend, and we explored how our online behaviors can impact others.

For the next week, notice when others, including yourself, may be distracted by a screen and not paying attention to what's happening around them. For example, watch people in restaurants, bus or carpool lines, stores, or other public places. If you're being ignored, pay close attention to how you feel about being second in line to a device. Take it one step further—think about how you want to do things differently.

# CYBERSECURITY AND ONLINE SAFETY

# Cybersecurity: Protecting Your Information

## MIND MAP

On the board, draw a mind map and ask students to consider ways to *protect their information* when they are online.

## ASCA® STANDARDS

- **B-SMS 1.** Responsibility for self and actions

- **B-SMS 2.** Self-discipline and self-control

- **B-SMS 9.** Personal safety skills

- **B-SS 5.** Ethical decision-making and social responsibility

## DIRECTIONS

Review the Group Expectations before reviewing the Mind Map. Then, read the Lesson Introduction and talk through the Key Terms for the lesson. Ask the Ice Breaker Questions and complete the Activity. Students can then work in pairs to craft their responses to the Discussion Questions or share with the whole group. Complete the Skill Builder and What Would You Do? game, as time allows. Be sure to complete the Closing Considerations with each lesson.

## LESSON INTRODUCTION

Does anyone know your password or passcode for any website or social media app? What about logging into your laptop or, better yet, your cell phone? This week, we will investigate whether you are using all the necessary precautions to protect your information online. We'll discuss privacy settings, securing your identity, and the do's and don'ts for keeping yourself safe when you're on your devices. All these areas fall under the topic of cybersecurity, and they are things everyone should be doing to protect themselves online.

## LESSON OBJECTIVES

During this session, participants will:

1. Evaluate their password management practices and what personal information they share on various sites.

2. Learn about cybersecurity and its importance in safeguarding personal information and identities.

3. Understand the impact of their online activity on personal security.

4. Develop skills to manage their online presence responsibly.

## KEY TERMS

Below are some common terms used throughout this chapter.

- **Cybercrime** is criminal activity carried out on a computer or networked device.

- **Cybersecurity** is protecting devices, data, and networks from unauthorized access or criminal activity.

- **Internet Protocol (IP) Address** is the unique identifying number attached to a known device. An IP address reveals the location of the device when it's connected to the internet. The IP address also reveals what types of sites have been visited.

- **Multi-factor authentication** is an additional security method that requires users to provide more than one form of identification to access information, often with an email or text sent to the user's device to verify.

- **Virtual Private Network (VPN)** protects users by encrypting their data and hiding their IP address.

Engage students in the following discussion. Ask follow-up questions to encourage participation.

- If you could provide three tips to a younger kid about how to treat others online, what three things would you tell them, and why do you believe it's important they know this information?

## ACTIVITY

# Cybersecurity Quiz

Cybersecurity is of the utmost importance, and minor changes to your accounts can make a big difference. How secure is your online information? Let's take the **Cybersecurity Quiz** to see how protected you are online.

1. Do you use the same or a similar password for your accounts?

2. Do you use multi-factor authentication to access your accounts?

3. Do you have an antivirus software package on your device?

4. Do you use public (free) Wi-Fi?

5. Do you open emails or attachments from people or places you don't know?

6. Do you use a virtual private network (VPN) on your device to encrypt your personal data and mask your IP address?

7. Are your devices locked down by a personal identification number (PIN), fingerprint, or voice recognition?

8. Do you share publicly on your social media sites?

Use the **Cybersecurity Quiz Answer Sheet** to tally up scores.

- **If you scored 5–8,** your information is at risk, and you need to take action so hackers or scammers can't compromise your personal information easily.

- **If you scored 3–4,** you're doing a pretty good job protecting yourself, but there is room for improvement.

- **If you scored 1–2,** you are aware of protecting yourself online but can still add more protection layers to secure your data.

- **If you didn't receive any points,** way to go! You are protecting yourself and your information.

## TALKING POINTS

- Use a **different password for your online accounts**.

- Use a **variety of capital letters, numbers, and symbols** when setting up your passwords.

- Use **different passwords on your devices and sites**. If hackers can get into one site with your password, they'll use their programs to see if they can access other accounts with that same password.

- **Don't open emails from unknown senders**, and don't open attachments or click on links from accounts you don't know. Doing so can expose your device to malware, which is software that can harm your device and leave you susceptible to identity theft or destructive viruses.

- When on social media, do **not open links from unfamiliar sites**.

- Passwords alone won't protect you. Adding **multi-factor authentication** helps you verify your identity and boosts your safety.

- **Antivirus software programs** help provide additional security to your personal information.

- Set up multiple ways to access your device. **Keep your device locked and secured by PINs, fingerprints, or facial recognition.** Do not share PINs with anyone other than your parent/guardian.

- **Do not post your whereabouts, school information, date of birth, home address, or other sensitive information about yourself.** Too much information can put you in jeopardy because people, such as trolls, hackers, or scammers who don't have your best intentions in mind, can use this information to harm you.

- **Be careful using Wi-Fi in public places.** The freedom of free Wi-Fi may come at a hefty price. Hackers go after easy targets. So, the less protected your systems are, the more susceptible you are to being hacked. Hackers conveniently put themselves between you and the hotspot in public places, intercepting your information. Once they have access, they can freely come and go from your system.

- Remember to **log off all devices** when you are finished.

# Find Me If You Can

Today, we will pair up and do an investigative search on one another. We will use our devices to gather as much information as possible on our partners to see how protected they are online. See if you can find out where they live, where they go to school, and what restaurant they visited most recently. You can begin your search with their name and city.

After some time has passed, encourage group members to report on how much they found out about their partner. Here are some questions they could ask:

- What personal information did they discover?
- Were there tagged photos or other information about them that could compromise their safety?
- How long did it take to find out information on their partner?
- Was the search easy because there was a lot of information about them online?

Allow the group to share and reflect on the experience and explore better ways to protect themselves and their information.

## WHAT WOULD YOU DO?

Work through the following dilemma with students.

*Michael is playing an MMO game with a friend he met online. They have much in common, such as favorite foods, music, and sports teams. They've been chatting for a while but only know each other by their screen names. Michael is known as "Blaze," and his new friend is "Ace." One day, Ace was chatting with Blaze and started asking him for more information, such as his name, birthday, and school name. Blaze didn't think twice and started answering Ace's questions. Ironically, Ace stated his birthday was the same as Blaze's! What a coincidence! Next, Ace asked for Blaze's real name, and he shared that, too. The more they talked, the more they had in common. It was too good of a friendship to be true! Blaze had never found someone like Ace before. Pause...*

Discussion Questions:

- What are some considerations that Michael should consider in this interaction?
- What are the risks associated with sharing personal information?
- Can Ace track down Michael based on the information provided? Explain.

## CLOSING CONSIDERATIONS

Today, we discussed online safety and ways to keep our information secure. As you leave today's session, consider what you must do to better protect your online information. Go home, review your social media accounts, and examine the privacy settings to ensure they are set up appropriately. Safeguard your information by securing your identity and personal details. By doing so, you can become more cyber secure.

# CHAPTER 4

# CYBERSECURITY: HACKING, PHISHING, AND SCAMS

## MIND MAP

On the board, draw a mind map and ask students to consider *online risks*.

## ASCA® STANDARDS

- **B-SMS 2.** Self-discipline and self-control

- **B-SMS 6.** Ability to identify and overcome barriers

- **B-SMS 9.** Personal safety skills

- **B-SS 5.** Ethical decision-making and social responsibility

Review the Group Expectations before reviewing the Mind Map. Then, read the Lesson Introduction and talk through the Key Terms for the lesson. Ask the Ice Breaker Questions and complete the Activity. Students can then work in pairs to craft their responses to the Discussion Questions or share with the whole group. Complete the Skill Builder and What Would You Do game, as time allows. Be sure to complete the Closing Considerations with each lesson.

## LESSON INTRODUCTION

Today, we will delve into widespread cybercrimes to which we are all susceptible. Cybercrimes, a.k.a. crimes on the internet, are on the rise. Sadly, young people who are on their devices and have a more detailed online presence are vulnerable to these crimes. So, what can you do to protect yourself and ensure that you don't become the victim of a cybercrime?

## LESSON OBJECTIVES

During this session, participants will:

1. Learn about cybercrimes, particularly those targeting young people.

2. Explore different cybercrimes, including hacking, phishing (fake emails or websites), and scams (online fraud), and understand their impact and consequences.

3. Recognize common signs of cybercrimes, such as suspicious emails, requests for personal information, and fraudulent websites or apps.

4. Learn what to do if online information has been targeted or compromised.

## KEY TERMS

Below are some common terms used throughout this chapter.

- **Hacking** is unauthorized access to data on a computer or digital device.

- **Phishing** is an attempt to trick recipients in order to steal their information. It often occurs when you receive a text or email message from what appears to be a reputable source. For example, the message looks like it's from your bank requesting more information. One simple but sometimes effective way to check is to look at the URL attached to the email by hovering over it to see if the link goes where it claims to go. If you aren't sure, you can use phishing verification tools to find out if it's a reported and known phishing link.

- **Scams** occur when someone uses you to obtain personal, financial, and/or other sensitive information or directly steal your money.

## ICEBREAKER

Engage students in the following discussion. Ask follow-up questions to encourage participation.

- Share an experience you or someone you know had with hacking, phishing, or scamming.

## ACTIVITY

# Think About It

Work through the questions with students and use the talking points to enrich teachable moments.

- **What are the chances one of your accounts will be hacked?**
  *Talking points:* On average, 97 cybercrimes occur every hour, which breaks down to one cybercrime every 37 seconds.[3] Unfortunately, this number is low because not all cybercrimes get reported.

- **How do you investigate apps before downloading them?**
  *Talking points:* Before downloading an application, check the permissions and review the required information before installing it on your device. Also, review others' experiences by reading their comments. Lastly, use antivirus software on your device because it may help detect harmful applications before downloading them.

- **If you believe you are being scammed, hacked, or blackmailed online, what should you do?**
  *Talking points:* If this happens to you, notify a trusted adult immediately. Once someone has access to your device, other information can become compromised, as hackers now have a back door into your information. Also, cybercriminals may exploit you based on what they find on your device. Don't let their scare tactics keep you from getting help.

## SKILL BUILDER

# Internet Crimes

Pair up students and tell them to go on an investigative dive using the internet to search for internet crimes involving hacking, phishing, or online scams.

Ensure all subgroups find a different story so there is more to share when they gather back in the large group. After 10–15 minutes, have them report on what they found, the consequences to the perpetrators and those victimized, and what precautionary measures could have been taken. This can help students avoid future cybercrimes like the one they found.

## WHAT WOULD YOU DO?

Work through the following dilemma with students.

*Jamie, a friend of yours, is incredibly tech-savvy. She is online for hours on end. One day, you are over at her house, and she shows you what she's been doing. She opened a forum where people were sharing information about hacking into sites and seeing people's personal information. Jamie swore you to secrecy but shared with you that she could make a lot of money if she sold the information. You are shocked at what Jamie tells you. You have heard stories where teen hackers have been caught and faced significant legal consequences for stealing data. Jamie looks like she is in over her head, but you can't reason with her that what she's doing isn't a good idea. She's too focused on the financial gain. You know you need to do something fast, but you don't want Jamie to get into legal trouble.*

Discussion Questions:

- What do you do?

- Who do you tell Jamie?

- Now that you know, if you don't tell and Jamie gets caught, could you get into trouble, too?

## CLOSING CONSIDERATIONS

Today, we delved into three prevalent cybercrimes: hacking, phishing, and scams. Recognizing and circumventing threats can ensure cybersecurity. By taking precautionary steps when we are online, we can create a safer digital space.

# CHAPTER 5

# CYBERSECURITY: SEXTORTION AND SEXTING

## MIND MAP

On the board, draw a mind map and ask students to consider online *boundaries and safety*.

## ASCA® STANDARDS

- **B-SMS 2.** Self-discipline and self-control

- **B-SMS 9.** Personal safety skills

- **B-SS 5.** Ethical decision-making and social responsibility

- **B-SS 9.** Social maturity and behaviors appropriate to the situation and environment

## DIRECTIONS

Review the Group Expectations before reviewing the Mind Map. Then, read the Lesson Introduction and talk through the Key Terms for the lesson. Ask the Ice Breaker Questions and complete the Activity. Students can then work in pairs to craft their responses to the Discussion Questions or share with the whole group. Complete the Skill Builder and What Would You Do? game, as time allows. Be sure to complete the Closing Considerations with each lesson.

## LESSON INTRODUCTION

In addition to the cybercrimes we have already discussed, there are two more that warrant a deeper discussion: sexting and sextortion. The FBI has seen a significant increase in the number of cases involving young people being threatened and coerced into sending sexually explicit images online (sexting) and people extorting them because of those photos (sextortion). Extortion of any nature is an illegal activity and needs to be reported. Many people think they'd never send sexual pictures to another person, and that may be true, but odds are they know someone who would, and in doing so, may end up in big trouble. Also, these pictures risk being released on the dark web and being used by cybercriminals for criminal activity. In today's lesson, we'll discuss ways you can help them.

## LESSON OBJECTIVES

During this session, participants will:

1. Learn about sextortion (blackmail involving sexual content) and sexting (sending or receiving sexually explicit messages or images).

2. Examine real-life scenarios involving sextortion and sexting to understand the risks and consequences associated with these activities.

3. Identify warning signs of online coercion, such as receiving unsolicited requests for explicit images or threats related to compromising materials.

4. Explore strategies to protect themselves and others from falling victim to sextortion, including managing privacy settings, refusing requests for explicit content, and seeking help if threatened.

## KEY TERMS

Below are some common terms used throughout this chapter.

- The **Dark Web** is a secretive collective of internet sites only accessible through a special web browser.

- **Sexting** is sending, receiving, or forwarding sexual messages through technology.

- **Sextortion** is threatening to release private information unless you provide a sexual photo, sexual favors, or money.

Engage students in the following discussion. Ask follow-up questions to encourage participation.

- Share any stories you've heard or come across about sextortion or sexting.

# The Real Stories of Sextortion

Read through the following sextortion scams and allow time after each story for students to reflect on how predators and criminals target young people. Lead them in a discussion about what makes them particularly vulnerable to sextortion.

**Ryan's Story:**

*Unfortunately, there have been too many cases of youth who have died by suicide after being sexually extorted. One mother, Pauline Stewart, shares her son's story through the San Jose Police Department via the Office of Juvenile Justice and Delinquency Prevention to warn parents of the dangers of social media and scammers.[4] Stewart's son, Ryan, was a victim of sextortion during his senior year of high school. An online scammer pretended to be a young girl interested in Ryan. The cybercriminal sent an explicit photo and asked Ryan to send one in return. When he did, the scammer threatened to share the image on social media if Ryan didn't send money. Fearing for his reputation, Ryan sent the money. Then, when the scammers demanded more money than Ryan could access, they urged him to end his life. In a note Ryan left behind, he described his embarrassment.*

**Gavin's Story:**

*Another teen, Gavin Guffey, died by suicide at age 17 after being misled and sextorted online. His father, a South Carolina State Representative, pushed for a state law called "Gavin's Law." This law establishes sexual extortion as a felony offense and an aggravated felony if the victim is a minor or vulnerable adult or if the victim suffers bodily injury or death directly related to the crime. Under this bill, scammers can be sentenced to up to twenty years in prison if the victim of sextortion is a minor.[5]*

# Safety Tips for Peers

Have students work together to create a schoolwide public service announcement about protecting themselves online and what to do if they ever find themselves in a dangerous or compromising situation.

Pair students up and assign them a subtopic, or let them pick the area they most want to address. Tell them their PSA should be no more than 2-3 minutes long. Encourage students to utilize online video creators to craft their announcements. They can use a shared document or virtual whiteboard to brainstorm ideas for the infomercial. Once students complete the final product, have them share it aloud with other group members. Think about ways you can use these PSA messages to promote awareness. For example, can The PSAs air across the school announcements, be shared during homeroom, or be placed on the website? Encourage students to think of this project as a way to give back to their school community.

Principles to include in the PSA:

- Do not send compromising images of yourself to anyone.

- Avoid clicking on email links or opening attachments received from people you do not know.

- Turn off your electronic devices and web cameras when not in use. Also, webcams or recording devices can be hacked and activated remotely, so cover your webcam lens when it's not in use.

- Do not interact with people online if you do not know them personally.

- Do not share sensitive personal information that can identify you.

## WHAT WOULD YOU DO?

Work through the following dilemma with students.

*Emily had become online friends with a guy named Nathan. She talked with Nathan for weeks and was beginning to like him. One night, Nathan asked Emily to send him a semi-nude photo of herself. He promised it was for his eyes only. Going against her best judgment, Emily decided to send the picture. A few hours later, Nathan started sending her messages that unless she sent him money, he was going to "ruin" her by making her picture public and sending it out to her friends and family. Emily was frightened and didn't know what to do. She also didn't have the amount of money Nathan asked for. She was terrified and scared that she would get into trouble if she told anyone what happened.*

Discussion Questions:

- What should Emily do in this situation?

- Should she keep this information to herself?

- Who should she tell?

## CLOSING CONSIDERATIONS

For the past three sessions, we have discussed cybercrimes and cybersecurity. We have uncovered the hidden dangers of not protecting ourselves online and making decisions that could put us in harm's way. Think about how you can better protect yourself online and what you can do to help protect those you care for, too.

# SECTION THREE

# EMOTIONAL SAFETY

# Emotional Well-Being

## MIND MAP

On the board, draw a mind map and ask students to consider how technology can impact *our emotional well-being*.

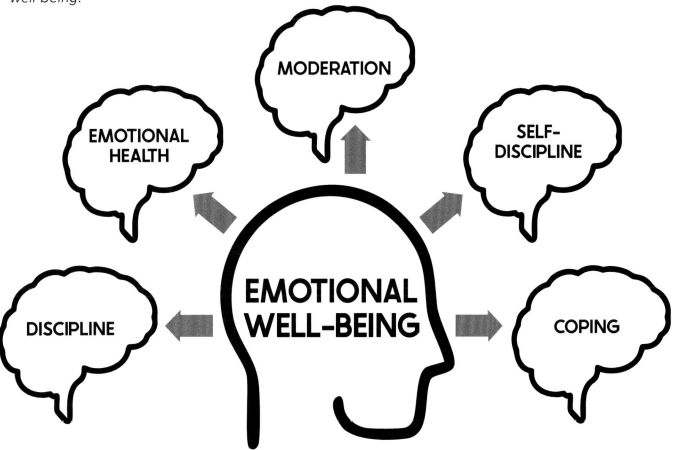

## ASCA® STANDARDS

- **B-SMS 1.** Responsibility for self and actions

- **B-SMS 2.** Self-discipline and self-control

- **B-SMS 4.** Delayed gratification for long-term rewards

- **B-SMS 6.** Ability to identify and overcome barriers

- **B-SMS 7.** Effective coping skills

## DIRECTIONS

Review the Group Expectations before reviewing the Mind Map. Then, read the Lesson Introduction and talk through the Key Terms for the lesson. Ask the Ice Breaker Questions and complete the Activity. Students can then work in pairs to craft their responses to the Discussion Questions or share with the whole group. Complete the Skill Builder and What Would You Do? game, as time allows. Be sure to complete the Closing Considerations with each lesson.

## LESSON INTRODUCTION

Excessive dependence on technology can impact our physical and emotional health significantly. Too much screen time has been linked with anxiety, depression, and other mental health conditions. Did you know that social media platforms are designed to be addictive and that how they make us feel can reinforce our use of them even more? Social media has a reinforcing nature. Positive feedback and likes encourage us to post more on these sites, and when this happens, our brain reward center becomes stimulated. The brain's reward center is a neural network of interconnected structures that regulate pleasure and motivate behavior. Today's session will explore how the internet can impact your mental health and how too much of a good thing may not be good.

## LESSON OBJECTIVES

During this session, participants will:

1. Examine how technology can affect emotional well-being, including its potential association with anxiety, depression, and self-esteem issues.

2. Analyze common online triggers, such as seeking validation through positive likes or comments.

3. Develop self-awareness regarding emotional responses to online interactions and learn strategies to manage and regulate these emotions effectively.

4. Establish expectations for positive online behavior, including empathy, respect, and proactive communication, to create a supportive online community.

## KEY TERMS

Below are some common terms used throughout this chapter.

- **Emotional Well-being is** being able to manage and cope with adversity and challenges healthily.

- **Moderation** is the avoidance of excess.

- **Supportive Online Community** is an online space where people with shared interests or experiences connect and feel a sense of belonging and kindredship.

Engage students in the following discussion. Ask follow-up questions to encourage participation.

- Draw the emoji you use most often. Share it with the group and discuss what you believe your emoji says about your personality.

**ACTIVITY**

# Moderation

In December 1927, *The Daily Mail* newspaper of Hull, England, printed an editor's column that listed a collection of items, including the following quote:

*"Be moderate in everything including moderation."*[6]

**What do you think this quote means? How can it be applied to technology?**

Studies have shown that teens who spend more than three hours on social media a day are more likely to have poor mental health and low self-esteem.[7]

- Does this information surprise you? Why or why not?
- Why do you believe people who spend more time gaming or on social media are more prone to mental health issues?[8]
- What advice would you give to people who are over-reliant on technology?
- What can you do to bring more moderation into your life?
- Why do so many young people check their devices because they fear missing out (FOMO) on something?

**SKILL BUILDER**

# Just Notice

In this exercise, think about times you are on your device and times you are not, and then *notice how things are different*. For the next week, closely monitor your surroundings and pay attention to your moods, feelings, and emotions online and offline. We'll discuss this in our next session.

Questions:

- Compare and contrast how you feel when you are online for hours versus doing something in person with your friends or being outdoors.
- Why do you think spending an hour with a friend in person is better than communicating with them only online?

- How do you feel about shopping online versus visiting a store with a friend or family member?

- When have you experienced frustration, fear, stress, anxiety, or worry about the reactions of others on social media?

- Do you feel compelled to reply to all texts or comments on sites, or does responding to every little thing feel like a chore? Explain.

## WHAT WOULD YOU DO?

Work through the following dilemma with students.

*Charlotte was spending a boring weekend at home with nothing to do because her friends were either out of town or doing something with their families, or so she thought. While scrolling through her social media, she noticed her friends posting pictures of hanging out at another friend's house. They lied to her. She felt rejected, hurt, and angry.*

Discussion Questions:

- What advice would you give to Charlotte?

- Would you take this advice yourself? Explain.

- Have you ever been in a similar situation? If so, how did you handle it?

## CLOSING CONSIDERATIONS

In today's session, we explored how important it is to notice how we feel online and how too much of a good thing can be harmful. Social media can lead to self-doubt, feelings of low self-worth, and jealousy, especially when people only post the highlights of their lives, prompting us to compare our lives to theirs. If you want to feel better online and offline, use your devices in moderation and engage in the activities you enjoy offline, too!

# Being Kind Online

## MIND MAP

On the board, draw a mind map and ask students to consider *being kind online*.

SELF-CONTROL · RESPECT · GRATITUDE · EMPATHY · KINDNESS · ADVOCACY

## ASCA® STANDARDS

- **B-SMS 1.** Responsibility for self and actions
- **B-SMS 2.** Self-discipline and self-control
- **B-SMS 6.** Ability to identify and overcome barriers
- **B-SS 1.** Effective oral and written communication skills and listening skills
- **B-SS 2.** Positive, respectful, and supportive relationships with students who are like and different from them
- **B-SS 3.** Positive relationships with adults to support success
- **B-SS 4.** Empathy
- **B-SS 8.** Advocacy skills for self and others and ability to assert self, when necessary

## DIRECTIONS

Review the Group Expectations before reviewing the Mind Map. Then, read the Lesson Introduction and talk through the Key Terms for the lesson. Ask the Ice Breaker Questions and complete the Activity. Students can then work in pairs to craft their responses to the Discussion Questions or share with the whole group. Complete the Skill Builder and What Would You Do? game, as time allows. Be sure to complete the Closing Considerations with each lesson.

## LESSON INTRODUCTION

About 50% of youth have reported being cyberbullied or harassed online. Those most impacted by this behavior are females and LBGTQ+ individuals.[9] Being cyberbullied can have profound effects on a young person's well-being. Youth who report being cyberbullied report higher levels of anxiety, depression, and suicidal ideation. Today, we will explore the ever-concerning issue of cyberbullying and harassment and discuss the importance of kindness, empathy, and respect for differences.

## LESSON OBJECTIVES

During this session, participants will:

1. Recognize that online behavior has real-world consequences and impacts others, just like face-to-face interactions.

2. Learn the importance of empathy and respect for differences in online communication and understand how considering others' perspectives can lead to healthier interactions.

3. Explore strategies for communicating online, including using positive language, avoiding offensive or hurtful comments, and considering the impact of their words on others.

4. Practice ways to promote kindness and positivity in online communities, such as complimenting others, offering support, and standing up against bullying.

## KEY TERMS

Below are some common terms used throughout this chapter.

- **Cyberbullying** occurs when a person uses electronic devices to share hurtful and untrue information about another person online repetitively.

- **Harassment** is offensive and demeaning behaviors aimed at harming, demeaning, or humiliating another person.

Engage students in the following discussion. Ask follow-up questions to encourage participation.

**Recap from the last session:**

- Last week, you were asked to be aware of your moods, feelings, and emotions when you were online and offline. What did you notice?

*(This is a great opportunity to share the differences you've personally observed between interacting online and offline.)*

**Moving onto today's session:**

- If you could give three tips to a younger kid about how to treat others online, what advice would you share?

## ACTIVITY

# Yep, That Happened...

Ask participants to respond to the following questions.

- **What is the most humiliating or hurtful experience you or someone you know has encountered online?** For each experience students share, discuss how that situation could make someone feel and discuss ways to manage that situation constructively.

- Maya Angelou once said, *"Be a rainbow in somebody else's cloud."* **What do you believe this quote means? How can we apply this quote to our online behavior?**

## SKILL BUILDER

# A Call to Action for Online Kindness

Here are some guidelines to keep in mind while online to ensure your safety and maintain sensitivity toward others' feelings:

- Remember, **words can have consequences**. Think before you post a comment or information about others online.

- **Refrain from sharing private or sensitive material online**, whether a picture or someone's post.

- If you see someone else acting unkindly, **report and block them**.

- **Respect others' privacy.** Just as you have learned not to share information about yourself, do not share anything about others.

- **Support those who are being treated unkindly**. Send a message of support or offer some kind words. A little kindness can go a long way.

- **Watch your tone**. Think about how your message sounds before posting. If you're unsure whether you should post, odds are you shouldn't. Also, it's good to put some space between typing and sending when addressing difficult situations or topics. So, step away for a while and then go back and re-read what you wrote. You may realize it comes across differently than you intended.

- What would you add to this list?

Let's develop a schoolwide ad that promotes online kindness in our community.

Today, we will create a poster, bulletin board, flyer, newsletter, t-shirt, or any other ideas to promote our online kindness campaign. We will collectively work together to answer this call to action and then discuss ways of promoting our campaign in our school.

## WHAT WOULD YOU DO?

Work through the following dilemma with students.

*Aidan hated going to school. He didn't have any friends because the people he thought were his friends turned on him. They teased and mocked him in the halls, cafeteria, and online. They kept messaging, threatening, and embarrassing him online. Aidan had no idea what he did to bring all this on, but he just wanted it to stop. He hated school and even stopped going to the cafeteria for lunch. He also didn't want to tell anyone because he believed it would only make it worse for him if he did.*

Discussion Questions:

- Is Aidan being bullied?

- Is he being cyberbullied?

- What actions would you recommend Aidan take in this situation?

## CLOSING CONSIDERATIONS

Whenever we are online, our behavior can help or harm another person. Think of how you would like to be treated and treat others with the same courtesy. Today, we discussed ways our words can hurt or help others.

# ONLINE PREDATORS

## MIND MAP

On the board, draw a mind map and ask students to consider how they can protect themselves from *online predators*.

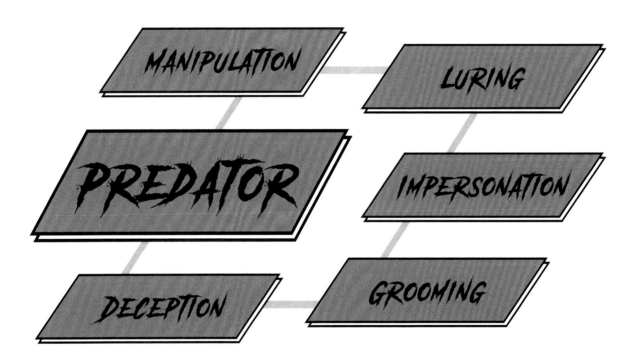

## ASCA® STANDARDS

- **B-SMS 1.** Responsibility for self and actions
- **B-SMS 2.** Self-discipline and self-control
- **B-SMS 6.** Ability to identify and overcome barriers
- **B-SMS 9.** Personal safety skills
- **B-SS 8.** Advocacy skills for self and others and ability to assert self, when necessary
- **B-SS 9.** Social maturity and behaviors appropriate to the situation and environment

## DIRECTIONS

Review the Group Expectations before reviewing the Mind Map. Then, read the Lesson Introduction and talk through the Key Terms for the lesson. Ask the Ice Breaker Questions and complete the Activity. Students can then work in pairs to craft their responses to the Discussion Questions or share with the whole group. Complete the Skill Builder and What Would You Do? game, as time allows. Be sure to complete the Closing Considerations with each lesson.

## LESSON INTRODUCTION

Many people your age have online friendships or even more serious relationships, but how do you know if the person is who they say they are? For example, what if they are an online predator, someone who uses the internet to harm youth for abuse, usually sexual and exploitative purposes? According to the Pew Research Center, there are approximately 500,000 online predators active each day.[10] These predators use social media, online chats, and other forums to create phony relationships, engage in catfishing, and sexually groom their prey. Knowing their tactics and how to ensure you don't fall victim to online predators is the topic of today's session.

## LESSON OBJECTIVES

During this session, participants will:

1. Explore the nature of online relationships, including friendships and romantic connections formed through electronic platforms.

2. Identify warning signs of online predators, such as requests for personal information, attempts to meet in person, and/or manipulative or coercive behaviors.

3. Develop strategies for maintaining safety in online relationships, including setting boundaries, verifying identities, and being cautious about sharing personal information.

4. Analyze and discuss real-life scenarios involving online relationships and safety concerns.

5. Apply critical thinking skills to evaluate risks and make well-informed decisions.

## KEY TERMS

Below are some common terms used throughout this chapter.

- **Catfishing** occurs when a person creates a fictional persona or fake identity on a social media network to deceive someone and/or commit fraud.

- **Online Predator** is an internet user who exploits minors for sexual and violent purposes.

- **Sexual Grooming** is a behavior used to establish an online relationship with a vulnerable person, like a minor, with the purpose of sexual exploitation.

Engage students in the following discussion. Ask follow-up questions to encourage participation.

- What is an online predator, and why is it important to know about them?
- How vulnerable do you believe young people are to these crimes?
- What makes young people susceptible to these criminals?

## ACTIVITY

# Debunking Predator Stereotypes

Ask the students, **"When you think of an online predator, what comes to mind?"** Allow students space to discuss their stereotypes surrounding online predators.

Share the following information with students and discuss each point:

- 16% of U.S. youth have experienced at least one type of online sexual abuse before the age of 18.[11]
- 75% of children are willing to share personal information online about themselves and their families in exchange for goods and services.[12]
- At 60%, the most common goal of internet predators is to obtain sexually explicit content of children.[13]
- One study found that 77% of targets for online predators were age 14 or older.[14]
- Teens are more likely to receive requests to talk about sexual things online from other teens or young adults (ages 18 to 25) than they are from older adults.[15]
- The small percentage of adults who do seek out relationships with teens online are usually up-front about their age and their sexual interests.[16]
- 98% of predators are people children don't know in real life.[17]

## SKILL BUILDER

# Investigating Online Predators

### Share This Information

Online predators are eagerly searching for their next vulnerable victim, and let's make sure that's not you. Did you know the ages most susceptible to these predators are between 12 and 17 years?[18] Most of their luring tactics occur in chatrooms or through instant messaging. It's common for predators to groom their victims by making teens believe they are a similar age, have similar likes, and understand them (the teens). Once the relationship is established, the hook is set. Then, the predators proceed to ask for more risky content or sexually explicit photos. They may even try to meet up with their victim. Only later does the victim find out it's not the person they thought it was. This whole experience can be dangerous and potentially life-threatening.

**Investigative Dig**

Partner up and look up online predator stories to share with the group.

Ensure all subgroups find a different story so there is more to share when they gather back in the large group. After 10-15 minutes, have them report what they found, the consequences to the victims, and what precautionary measures could have been taken to avoid online relationships like the ones they found.

**Create A Safety List**

Have the group work together and create an online relationship safety checklist that differentiates healthy online relationships from unhealthy ones, including both friendships and romantic interests. Encourage participants to write down at least ten healthy and ten unhealthy characteristics.

Using their list, engage the group in the following discussions:

- How do online relationships differ from in-person ones?

- What are the important qualities of a healthy online relationship?

- What are some characteristics of an unhealthy online relationship?

- How do you distinguish between a supportive and healthy online relationship and an unhealthy one?

- What would you do if you were in an unhealthy online relationship?

To enhance this activity, you could show characteristics of both types of relationships using movies or video clips.

## WHAT WOULD YOU DO?

Partner students up and allow them to **create their own What Would You Do? scenario** using catfishing or online predator situations. After ample time, ask each group to share their scenario with the larger group and discuss ways to identify online predators and how to stay safe.

## CLOSING CONSIDERATIONS

Today's session covered the important topic of online relationships and explored concepts such as catfishing and online predators. We examined important statistics and debunked myths about online predators. We even established a list of healthy versus unhealthy relationships. Remember, before sharing any information about yourself, make sure you genuinely know who you are communicating with online. It's not worth the risk of befriending someone you don't know. Please stay safe and make wise decisions so you don't become one of the statistics we discussed today.

# THE FUTURE OF TECHNOLOGY

# ARTIFICIAL INTELLIGENCE

## MIND MAP

On the board, draw a mind map and ask students to consider how they will use *Artificial Intelligence (AI)*.

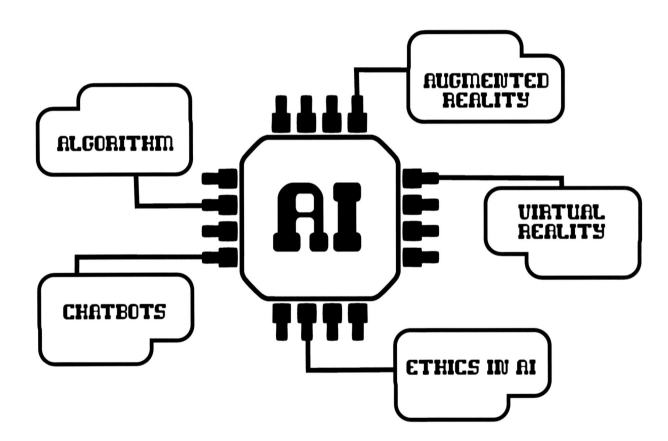

## ASCA® STANDARDS

- **B-SMS 1.** Responsibility for self and actions

- **B-SMS 2.** Self-discipline and self-control

- **B-SMS 3.** Independent work

## DIRECTIONS

Review the Group Expectations before reviewing the Mind Map. Then, read the Lesson Introduction and talk through the Key Terms for the lesson. Ask the Ice Breaker Questions and complete the Activity. Students can then work in pairs to craft their responses to the Discussion Questions or share with the whole group. Complete the Skill Builder and What Would You Do? game, as time allows. Be sure to complete the Closing Considerations with each lesson.

## LESSON INTRODUCTION

New innovations and apps hit the market daily, and we can become mesmerized by what they do. Take, for example, AI (Artificial Intelligence). In simple terms, AI is the science of having a machine perform tasks that typically require human intelligence, such as problem-solving and making decisions or judgments. As fascinating as this may sound, there are also some concerns with using AI that we need to discuss in today's session.

## LESSON OBJECTIVES

During this session, participants will:

1. Develop an understanding of artificial intelligence (AI), including its definition and examples of tasks it can perform that traditionally require human intelligence.

2. Explore real-world applications of AI across various industries, such as healthcare, transportation, finance, and entertainment.

3. Discuss ethical concerns related to the use of AI.

4. Analyze the societal impact of AI advancements, considering both positive effects (innovation) and potential negative consequences (ethical dilemmas).

## KEY TERMS

Below are some common terms used throughout this chapter.

- **Artificial Intelligence (AI)** occurs when a computer system performs tasks that require human intelligence.

- **Augmented Reality (AR)** is an interactive experience that combines the real world with computer-generated content.

- **Chatbots** are computer simulations created to engage in conversations with humans.

- **Extended Reality (XR)** is shorthand for augmented reality, visual reality,

- and mixed reality.

- **Humanoid** refers to a robot resembling a human form.

- **Virtual Reality (VR)** is using computer technology to simulate environments, scenes, and objects that appear real.

## ICEBREAKER

Engage students in the following questions. Ask follow-up questions to encourage participation.

- Imagine that you had an AI bot for an entire day. It would be your personal assistant. What would you have it do, and why did you choose those tasks?

## ACTIVITY

# Exploring a World with AI

Engage students in answering the following questions. Ask follow-up questions to encourage participation.

- When you think about artificial intelligence, what comes to mind?
- How would you define the following terms?
  - Augmented Reality
  - Chatbots
  - Humanoids
  - Extended Reality
  - Virtual Reality
- How do you think artificial intelligence will change how we live and operate in the world?
- In what ways do you believe AI will be helpful in the future?
- In what ways do you think it will be unhelpful?
- What are some things we can do to offset the negative impact of using AI?

## SKILL BUILDER

# Can You Stump AI?

In this activity, students will interact with an AI model and reflect upon its capabilities and implications.

Can you stump the computer by providing clues about a movie, song, or book? Let's see if we can throw AI off track by giving it only a few clues and then sitting back to see if the machine can outsmart the human. We'll begin by giving minimal clues to our AI prompter and then see how much information it requires to make an appropriate guess.

Example:

- "Guess the (movie, song, or book) that I will I describe in these four words (give four words to describe)."

- Human Prompt: Describe the movie with pink cars and plastic.
- Possible AI answer: AI: You might be thinking of "Barbie" (2023), which features a lot of pink and plastic elements, including cars."

Play several rounds of this activity so group members can see if they can trick the machine!

## WHAT WOULD YOU DO?

# AI-Generated What Would You Do?

For this activity, the author asked AI to generate some hypothetical AI dilemmas for students to work through. Here is what it provided, along with follow-up questions to ask students:[19]

- **Scenario 1:** A student uses an AI tool to create a deepfake video of a classmate and shares it on social media as a prank.
- **Scenario 2:** Someone uses an AI chatbot to impersonate a teacher and send misleading information to students.
- **Scenario 3:** A group of friends uses facial recognition software to track someone's movements without their consent.
- **Scenario 4:** A person uses AI to generate fake news articles that spread false information about a local event.

Discussion Questions:

- What are the potential consequences of this AI misuse for the people involved?
- Why might someone choose to misuse AI in this way?
- What ethical principles are being violated in this scenario?
- How could this situation be managed responsibly?

# Human-Generated What Would You Do?

The author wrote the following hypothetical dilemma for students to work through for this activity. Discuss the differences between the AI-generated dilemmas and the human written prompt. Have students work through the prompt below.

Kyle has a big paper due for his English class tomorrow. He has procrastinated and doesn't have time to write it. He saw a pop-up ad on his computer promoting a new AI app he could try for free. Kyle goes into the app and types in the prompts for the assignment, and the app writes a paper for him.

Discussion Questions:

- What should Kyle do with the AI-generated paper?
- What are the risks in keeping the AI-generated paper and passing it off as his own?

- What are the advantages of using AI for educational purposes?

- What are the disadvantages of using AI with your schoolwork?

Reminder: As fascinating as AI is, be careful about relying on it for schoolwork. Did you know there are apps that can detect whether AI has been used to generate reports, papers, and other assignments?

## CLOSING CONSIDERATIONS

What an exciting time we are living in. We use technology daily, exploring and uncovering new material our ancestors would never have dreamed possible, like AI. One important thing to note from today's session is that humans design AI; therefore, like many things, AI can be extremely exciting and helpful or devastating and harmful. It's up to us to decide the right way to use AI. Like other technology, AI is not scary or bad unless used to deceive, hurt, or harm others.

# MOVING FORWARD

## MIND MAP

On the board, draw a mind map and ask students to consider how they can use what they have learned in the group to be *upstanding digital citizens* while being safe in their online interactions.

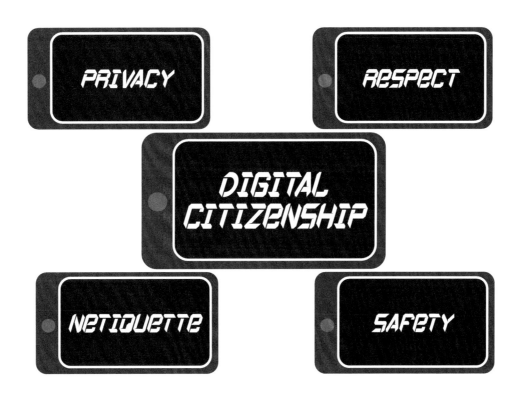

## ASCA® STANDARDS

- **B-SMS 1.** Responsibility for self and actions
- **B-SMS 2.** Self-discipline and self-control
- **B-SMS 8.** Balance of school, home, and community activities
- **B-SMS 9.** Personal safety skills
- **B-SMS 10.** Ability to manage transitions and adapt to change
- **B-SS 5.** Ethical decision-making and social responsibility
- **B-SS 9.** Social maturity and behaviors appropriate to the situation and environment

## DIRECTIONS

Review the Group Expectations before reviewing the Mind Map. Then, read the Lesson Introduction and talk through the Key Terms for the lesson. Ask the Ice Breaker Questions and complete the Activity. Students can then work in pairs to craft their responses to the Discussion Questions or share with the whole group. Complete the Skill Builder and What Would You Do? game, as time allows. Be sure to complete the Closing Considerations with each lesson.

## LESSON INTRODUCTION

Throughout our time together, we have been examining the importance of online safety, how we behave and interact with others online, and how to make smart, ethical choices as it relates to digital technology. We have worked through complex problems and discussed using our devices responsibly and in moderation. This week, we will discuss what being an upstanding digital citizen means (this lesson can help drive home the idea that we should continuously strive to be the person we want to be and manifest the change we want to see in the world).

## LESSON OBJECTIVES

During this session, participants will:

1. Understand the importance of digital literacy and digital citizenship, modeling online kindness by treating others with respect and empathy.

2. Reflect on the group experience and how online behaviors influence offline interactions, fostering a comprehensive understanding of digital and real-world dynamics.

3. Apply the knowledge and skills necessary to navigate digital environments responsibly, ethically, and safely while promoting positive digital citizenship.

## KEY TERMS

Below are some common terms used throughout this chapter.

- **Digital Citizenship** is our online behaviors and decisions that impact self, others, and our community. Good citizens engage with others respectfully and responsibly.

- **Digital Literacy** is the access and use of online resources.

- **Online Kindness** occurs when users treat others with dignity and respect, modeling courtesy and empathy to other users.

Engage students in the following discussion. Ask follow-up questions to encourage participation.

- What "vintage" devices do you still own and/or use?

- If you could change one thing about technology that could positively impact the world, what would you do?

- What are some ways technology has simplified life?

- How has technology made life more difficult or distracting?

## ACTIVITY

# Reflections and Takeaways

Now that we are closing our time with one another, let's pause and reflect on what we have learned throughout our journey. Using the **Reflections and Takeaways Worksheet**, write down at least three takeaways from all our group sessions. Next, write down some advice you'd give a peer about technology usage and online safety. Please think about what you are doing differently online now compared to when we first began the group. What led to this change?

Please allow ample time for participants to share their reflections and takeaways from the group experience.

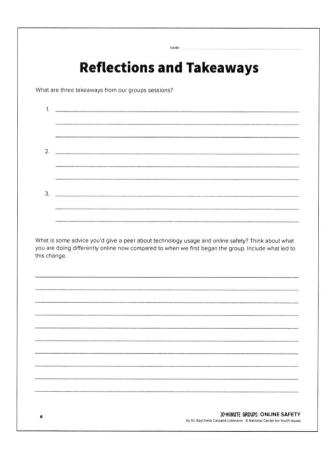

# For the Greater Good

Place students in groups and have them use technology to find sites where technology has been used to promote good, such as educational purposes, healthcare innovations, global connections, entertainment, and environmental sustainability.

Ensure all subgroups find different sites and explore diverse topics so there is more to share when they gather back in the large group. After 15-20 minutes, have them share their findings with the group. Some fun areas to explore include humanoids, augmented reality, Artificial Intelligence, and virtual reality.

## WHAT WOULD YOU DO?

As a part of our closure activity, let's explore how you would apply what you've learned through the group by working through the following scenarios together.

- What would you do if you came across a post where someone was being berated and personally attacked for sharing their opinion?

- What would you do if you knew the people engaging in the attacking behavior or, better yet, if you knew the person on the receiving end of the attacks?

- What would you do if you were the person being attacked, threatened, or blackmailed?

- What would you do if your friend secretly shared that they met someone online and planned to sneak out to meet them in person?

- What would you do if you noticed you are spending too much time on your device and your grades, sleep, and friendships begin to suffer?

## CLOSING CONSIDERATIONS

Over the past several weeks, we have engaged in a deep dive and explored:

- Digital awareness and managing screen time

- Cybersecurity

- Cybercrimes

- Online communication and behavior

- Future trends and ethical dilemmas

Ask students if they'd like to share anything before closing. Remind them of the final group next week where they will receive certificates of completion and celebrate their time together.

# Final Group Session

## LAST SESSION:
## Directions and Overview

This final session is recommended, but optional. You may conclude the group during the final lesson topic if time does not permit this final session.

**Directions:** This final session is more relaxed and carefree, allowing students to spend time with one another and process their feelings about the group's conclusion. Facilitators may provide structured games or allow students unstructured time together.

**Post-Group Expectations:** Many students will have grown accustomed to meeting with you and will need reassurance about what support will be available after the group's conclusion. Be sure to review the protocol for meeting with you once the group has concluded.

**Pre- and Post-Group Survey:** Ask students to complete the Post-Group Survey. Review the directions aloud. Discreetly ensure that all of the questions were answered when the forms are returned.

**Certificate of Completion:** Present each student with their own Certificate of Completion. You can have as much or as little fanfare around this experience as you would like. Playing a song and asking students to stand and clap for their peers creates lasting memories for the participants.

**Group Completion Letter:** Give each student their Group Completion Letter to share with their caregiver, notifying them that the group has officially ended.

**Group Conclusion:** Ask each student to share what, if anything, this group has meant to them. Model this activity by sharing your experience as the group's facilitator.

**Note to Facilitators:** If your district allows, concluding a group with a meal is often a fun experience for the students. If you are unable to purchase a meal with the district budget, perhaps students could bring their lunches. Be sure to have caregiver permission and be familiar with student's allergies before providing students with any food.

# Common Terms

Below are some common terms used throughout this book and in general. Hopefully, this glossary will help you understand and better navigate your discussions with students.

- **Artificial Intelligence (AI)** occurs when a computer system performs tasks that require human intelligence.

- **Augmented Reality (AR)** is an interactive experience that combines the real world with computer-generated content.

- **Catfishing** occurs when a person creates a fictional persona or fake identity on a social media network to deceive someone and/or commit fraud.

- **Chatbots** are computer simulations created to engage in conversations with humans.

- **Cyberbullying** occurs when a person uses electronic devices to share hurtful and untrue information about another person online repetitively.

- **Cybercrime** is a criminal activity conducted on a computer or networked device.

- The **Dark Web** is a secretive collective of internet sites only accessible through a special web browser.

- **Digital Citizenship** is our online behaviors and decisions that impact self, others, and our community. Good citizens engage with others respectfully and responsibly.

- **Digital Literacy** is the access and use of online resources.

- **Extended Reality (XR)** is shorthand for augmented reality, visual reality, and mixed reality.

- **Hacking** is unauthorized access to a computer system or network.

- **Humanoid** refers to a robot resembling a human form.

- **Internet Addiction**, also known as Problematic Internet Use (PIU), is the excessive use of the Internet that leads to adverse outcomes.

- **Internet Feeds** are data formats used to provide users with frequently updated content.

- **Internet Privacy** is the freedom of, or lack of intrusion into, online information.

- **Internet Protocol (IP) Address** is the unique identifying number attached to a known device. An IP address reveals the location of the device when it's connected to the internet. The IP address also reveals what types of sites have been visited.

- **Identity Theft**, also known as identity fraud, occurs when someone uses another person's information, such as name and identity number, without permission.

- **Malware** is software stored on a user's device without their consent that performs actions such as stealing personal information.

- **Nomophobia** is a fear of being without a cellular device or the internet.

- **Online Kindness** occurs when users treat others with dignity and respect, modeling courtesy and empathy to other users.

- **Online Identity**, also known as internet persona, is the sum of information we share and leave behind when we are online.

- An **Online Forum** is an online discussion site where people can hold conversations in the form of posted messages.

- **Personally Identifiable Information (PII)** is information that could be used to identify a person, such as a physical address, date of birth, email address, phone number, social security number, driver's license number, picture, or video or audio file that contains a person's image or voice.

- **Phishing** is the act of sending messages to trick you into providing your sensitive information to scammers.

- **Piracy** is the unauthorized use or reproduction of another's protected work.

- **Sexting** is sending, receiving, or forwarding sexual messages through technology.

- **Sextortion** is threatening to release private information unless you provide personal information such as a sexual photo, sexual favors, or money.

- **Total Internet Traffic** is the net flow of data within the entire internet.

- **Two-factor authentication (2FA)** is an additional security method that requires two forms of identification to access information, often with an email or text sent to the user's device to verify.

- **Virtual Private Network (VPN)** protects users by encrypting their data and hiding their IP address.

- **Virtual Reality (VR)** is using computer technology to simulate environments, scenes, and objects that appear real.

# RESOURCES

The following list of organizations, programs, descriptions, and links is not exhaustive, but it is designed to help educators quickly find information that will help them guide young people in navigating the internet and creating a positive online presence.

**Air Force Association — National CyberPatriot Education Program.**

This program offers free teaching modules to teach young people about online safety. There are opportunities to get your students and school involved in national competitions.

*https://www.uscyberpatriot.org/*

**American School Counselor Association (2021). ASCA® Student Standards: Mindsets & Behaviors for Student Success: K-12** college, career-and life-readiness standards for every student.

*https://www.schoolcounselor.org/getmedia/7428a787-a452-4abb-afec-d78ec77870cd/mindsets-behaviors.pdf*

**American School Counselor Association (2022). ASCA® Ethical Standards for School Counselors.**
*https://www.schoolcounselor.org/getmedia/44f30280-ffe8-4b41-9ad8-f15909c3d164/ethicalstandards.pdf*

**American School Counselor Association (2023). The school counselor and virtual school counselor. ASCA® position statements.**

*https://www.schoolcounselor.org/Standards-Positions/Position-Statements/ASCA®-Position-Statements/The-School-Counselor-and-Virtual-School-Counseling*

**Centers for Disease Control and Prevention (CDC)**

The CDC offers a wealth of data on youth behavior. The Youth Risk Behavior Survey polls thousands of U.S. high school students from public and private schools annually. You can use the data from the survey to increase awareness at faculty, parent, or community meetings.

*https://www.cdc.gov/healthyyouth/data/yrbs/results.htm*

**Common Sense Education**

Common Sense Education is a nonprofit with a K–12 curriculum on digital citizenship. The website has many resources for parents and educators to help teach digital citizenship.

*https://www.commonsense.org*

**Cyberbullying Research Center**

The Cyberbullying Research Center has a wealth of information about cyberbullying for parents, educators, mental health professionals, law enforcement, and youth.

*https://cyberbullying.org/*

**Family Online Safety Institute (FOSI)**

FOSI supports parents and educators in navigating the digital world, offering tips and resources related to social media use, digital safety, and more.

*https://www.fosi.org/*


**Federal Bureau of Investigation — Internet Cybercrime Reports**

The FBI releases a cybercrime report through its Internet Crime Complaint

Center (IC3). The report highlights trends and threats from American complaints. You can learn more about common cybercrimes in your state by visiting the site.

*https://www.ic3.gov/Home/AnnualReports*


**Federal Bureau of Investigation — Safe Online Surfing Program**

The FBI's Safe Online Surfing (SOS) program is developmentally appropriate for students in grades 3 to 8. The program offers lesson plans and games covering various digital citizenship topics.

*https://sos.fbi.gov/en/*


**Google — Be Internet Awesome**

The Be Internet Awesome downloadable curriculum is accompanied by an animated "Interland" game featuring music, 3D graphics, and colorful, fun geometric characters.

*https://beinternetawesome.withgoogle.com/en_us*


**iKeepSafe**

Google and iKeepSafe partnered to produce an interactive, hands-on digital citizenship curriculum. It gives students the opportunity to learn by doing. Each topic features videos, lesson plans, and student handouts.

*https://ikeepsafe.org/google-digital-literacy-citizenship-curriculum/*


**ISTE**

The International Society for Technology in Education (ISTE) is a nonprofit organization that helps educators use technology to revolutionize learning.

*https://iste.org/*


**National Integrated Cyber Education Research Center (NICERC)**

Through the U.S. Department of Homeland Security, NICERC offers K-12 cybersecurity curricula.

*https://niccs.cisa.gov/*


**National Suicide Prevention Lifeline: 988 Suicide and Crisis Lifeline**

*https://988lifeline.org/chat/*


**Stomp Out Bullying**

Resource for students to get help if they or someone they know is being bullied.

*https://www.stompoutbullying.org/*

**StopBullying.gov**

This governmental website provides information and resources on bullying.

*https://www.stopbullying.gov/*

**Suicide Crisis Line**

Resource for students to get help if they or someone they know is feeling helpless or having thoughts of self-harm or suicide.

Call or text 988.

*https://988lifeline.org*

**The Cybersecurity and Infrastructure Security Agency**

Offers a wide variety of information and resources to parents and educators.

*https://www.cisa.gov/*

**The Trevor Project**

Support for LGBTQ youth.

*https://www.thetrevorproject.org/*

# SMALL GROUP ACTION PLAN GUIDE

## GRADE LEVEL

The curriculum is ideal for 8th through 12th-grade students.

## GROUP TOPICS

Technology Use

Social Media: Pros and Cons

Cybersecurity: Protecting Your Information

Cybersecurity: Hacking, Phishing, and Scams

Cybersecurity: Sextortion and Sexting

Emotional Well-Being

Being Kind Online

Online Predators

Artificial Intelligence

Moving Forward

**10-12 Group Sessions**

**30 MIN**

## CURRICULUM & MATERIALS

**Curriculum:**

Use this *Online Safety Workbook* to facilitate your groups.

**Materials:**

Copies of the Surveys, Worksheets, pencils, scratch paper, electronic devices, and art supplies (markers, poster board, construction paper, etc.).

## ASCA® STUDENT BEHAVIOR STANDARDS  **16**

| | |
|---|---|
| B-SMS 1 | B-SS 3 |
| B-SMS 2 | B-SS 4 |
| B-SMS 3 | B-SS 5 |
| B-SMS 4 | B-SS 8 |
| B-SMS 6 | B-SS 9 |
| B-SMS 7 | |
| B-SMS 8 | |
| B-SMS 9 | |
| B-SMS 10 | |
| B-SS 1 | |
| B-SS 2 | |

## NUMBER OF STUDENTS AFFECTED

Small group is ideal for six to eight students. Fewer students if goals are related to behavioral issues.

*Online Safety* can be used for classroom lessons.

## PERCEPTION DATA

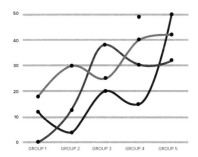

Use *Online Safety* survey data to create a visual representation of their progress using their pre- and post-group data.

## OUTCOME DATA

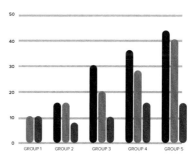

Use achievement, attendance, and behavior data to measure your students' progress. Compare pre- and post-group impacts.

# ONLINE SAFETY GROUP
# PERMISSION FORM

Greetings, Caregivers of: _____,

This form invites your student to attend an Online Safety Group. Our counseling department offers various services, including class lessons, small groups, and individual sessions with students. There are lots of reasons we invite students to attend groups. We invite students who might need help connecting with their peers, managing conflict or big emotions, improving their grades, or simply because their involvement will allow them to be more successful in their education journey. Your student is not in trouble, and being part of this group is meant to be a positive time for all attendees.

This group will focus on learning about navigating the online world safely and responsibly. We will discuss protecting personal information, avoiding online risks like scams and predators, understanding the impact of technology on emotional well-being, and more. Small groups are a fun way for students to learn valuable skills and connect with peers.

We will meet for approximately thirty minutes during the school day    times per week. I will work with your child's teacher to select an appropriate time that minimizes interruptions to their learning. When the student has completed all the group sessions, they will receive a Certificate of Completion.

I am excited to work with your child. Please don't hesitate to contact me with any questions or concerns.

Warm regards,

✂ -------------------------------------------------------------------------------------------

Please complete and return by: _____

**Student's Name:** _____

**Teacher's Name:** _____

☐  YES, I agree to allow my child to attend the Online Safety Group.

☐  NO, I do NOT agree to allow my child to attend the Online Safety Group.

_____
Signature of Caregiver

# ONLiNE SAFETY GROUP EXPECTATIONS

## CONFIDENTIALITY

In our group, we will keep what we talk about confidential. Confidentiality means keeping what is said in the group private and not discussing it outside of the group. We know that some things are private, and not everyone needs to know about them. However, because we are a group, we can't promise that everyone will keep what you say private, so please be mindful of what you share with the group. If you share that you plan to hurt yourself or someone else or that someone is hurting you, it is my duty to help keep you safe, which involves telling someone who needs to know and can keep you and others safe, as well.

## SAFETY

We create an environment of physical and emotional Safety. We don't make fun of others, but we watch out for each other.

## ASK FOR HELP WHEN NEEDED

This is a safe place to ask questions and receive help.

## LISTEN TO EACH OTHER

Listen from your heart. This is a space to be open, truthful, and respectful. Everyone belongs, and everyone will have a turn. When others are speaking, we can listen with full attention.

## HELP OTHERS WHEN WE CAN

It is okay to disagree, but we won't yell or call each other names.

We can support each other in keeping the space safe.

## DO OUR BEST

When we fully dive into listening and participating, we will get more out of the group and grow emotionally stronger.

## CREATE YOUR OWN

_____

_____

# Group Attendance Form

Group:_____ Day/Time:_____

| | 1 | 2 | 3 | 4 | 5 | 6 | 7 | 8 | 9 | 10 | 11 | 12 |
|---|---|---|---|---|---|---|---|---|---|---|---|---|
| DATE | | | | | | | | | | | | |
| | | | | | | | | | | | | |
| | | | | | | | | | | | | |
| | | | | | | | | | | | | |
| | | | | | | | | | | | | |
| | | | | | | | | | | | | |
| | | | | | | | | | | | | |
| | | | | | | | | | | | | |

SESSION 1

SESSION 2

SESSION 3

SESSION 4

SESSION 5

SESSION 6

SESSION 7

SESSION 8

SESSION 9

SESSION 10

SESSION 11

SESSION 12

# Group Attendance Form (Example)

**Group:** 5th Grade Lunch      **Day/Time:** Thursday@12:30

| | 1 | 2 | 3 | 4 | 5 | 6 | 7 | 8 | 9 | 10 | 11 | 12 |
|---|---|---|---|---|---|---|---|---|---|---|---|---|
| **DATE** | 3/2 | 3/9 | 3/16 | 3/23 | | | | | | | | |
| Jane/Ms. W's Class | X | X | X | X | X | X | X | X | X | X | X | X |
| George/Mr. Day's Class | X | X | | X | X | X | X | X | X | X | X | X |
| Sami/Ms. Smith's Class | X | X | X | X | X | X | X | X | X | X | X | X |
| John/Ms. Lee's Class | X | | X | X | X | X | X | X | X | X | X | X |
| Malik/Ms. Lee's Class | X | X | X | | X | X | | X | X | X | X | X |
| Prishna/Ms. Smith's Class | X | X | X | X | X | X | X | X | | X | | X |
| | | | | | | | | | | | | |

| | |
|---|---|
| **SESSION 1** | Intro/Surveys/Group Rules and Norms/ Discussed Expectations/ Connections |
| **SESSION 2** | Technology Use |
| **SESSION 3** | Social Media: Pros and Cons |
| **SESSION 4** | Cybersecurity: Protecting Your Information |
| **SESSION 5** | Cybersecurity: Hacking, Phishing, and Scams |
| **SESSION 6** | Cybersecurity: Sextortion and Sexting |
| **SESSION 7** | Emotional Well-Being |
| **SESSION 8** | Being Kind Online |
| **SESSION 9** | Online Predators |
| **SESSION 10** | Artificial Intelligence |
| **SESSION 11** | Moving Forward |
| **SESSION 12** | Check-Ins/ Post-Group Survey/ Process group experience & Certificates awarded |

# Pre- and Post-Group Survey

My name is:_____

Date:_____

# Online Safety Survey Pre-/Post-

On a scale of 1-5, with **1 being not at all** and **5 being completely**,
rate the following responses.

| | |
|---|---|
| I know how to safeguard my information online. | **1  2  3  4  5** |
| I can explain to someone what it means to be an upstanding digital citizen. | **1  2  3  4  5** |
| I know what sextortion is and how to protect myself from becoming a victim. | **1  2  3  4  5** |
| I can name various types of cybercrimes. | **1  2  3  4  5** |
| I know how to set up strong passwords and keep them secure. | **1  2  3  4  5** |
| I can identify phishing emails. | **1  2  3  4  5** |
| I know how to set up privacy settings. | **1  2  3  4  5** |
| I understand the consequences of unkind online behavior. | **1  2  3  4  5** |
| I can name the various types of artificial intelligence (AI). | **1  2  3  4  5** |
| I understand the importance of online safety. | **1  2  3  4  5** |
| I feel more confident about talking to someone if something happened online that made me feel unsafe. | **1  2  3  4  5** |

Anything else you would like to share about the group? Write it below.

_____

_____

# Post-Group Survey Results
# Online Safety Group Data

## GROUP GOAL:

## STUDENT STATEMENTS:

### GPA Results

Increase the total GPA following group intervention for group participation by ____%

____%

### Attendance Results

Decrease the number of absences by ____% following group intervention for group participants

____%

### Discipline Results

Decrease the number of conduct referrals by ____% following group intervention

____%

**STUDENTS ATTENDED**

**NUMBER OF SESSIONS**

**OVERALL IMPROVEMENT**

(See Formula Lower Right)

■ Pre-Group % True   ■ Post-Group % True

**AVERAGE SCORE**
5
4
3
2
1
0

- I know how to safeguard my information online.
- I can explain to someone what it means to be an upstanding digital citizen.
- I know what sextortion is and how to protect myself from becoming a victim.
- I can name various types of cybercrimes.
- I know how to set up strong passwords and keep them secure.
- I can identify phishing emails.
- I know how to set up privacy settings.
- I understand the consequences of unkind online behavior.
- I can name the various types of artificial intelligence (AI).
- I understand the importance of online safety.
- I feel more confident about talking to someone if something happened online that made me feel unsafe.

**OVERALL IMPROVEMENT FORMULA**

$$\left( \frac{\text{Post-Group Total - Pre-Group Total}}{\text{Pre-Group Total}} \right) \times 100$$

# Post-Group Survey Results (Example)
# Online Safety Group Data

## GROUP GOAL:

Reduce the number of discipline referrals by 10% for a group of six students who had more than three discipline referrals last year.

## STUDENT STATEMENTS:

"I learned how to protect my information online"

"I learned about cybersecurity and how to avoid hackers and scammers."

"I learned how to stay safe from online predators."

"I learned how to use technology responsibly and be a good digital citizen."

### GPA Results

Increase the total GPA following group intervention for group participation by **5** %

**5** %

### Attendance Results

Decrease the number of absences by **53** % following group intervention for group participants

**53** %

### Discipline Results

Decrease the number of conduct referrals by **42** % following group intervention

**42** %

**STUDENTS ATTENDED**

( **6** )

**NUMBER OF SESSIONS**

( **12** )

**OVERALL IMPROVEMENT**

( **57.89%** )

(See Formula Lower Right)

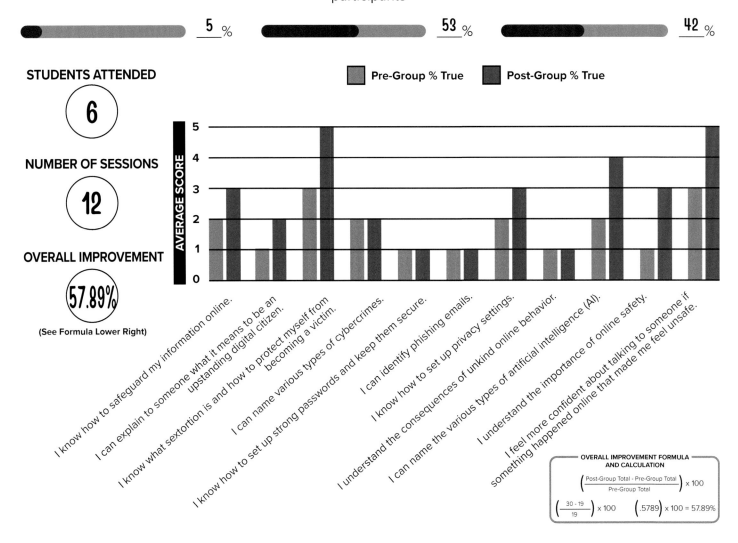

Pre-Group % True   Post-Group % True

AVERAGE SCORE

- I know how to safeguard my information online.
- I can explain to someone what it means to be an upstanding digital citizen.
- I know what sextortion is and how to protect myself from becoming a victim.
- I can name various types of cybercrimes.
- I know how to set up strong passwords and keep them secure.
- I can identify phishing emails.
- I know how to set up privacy settings.
- I understand the consequences of unkind online behavior.
- I can name the various types of artificial intelligence (AI).
- I understand the importance of online safety.
- I feel more confident about talking to someone if something happened online that made me feel unsafe.

**OVERALL IMPROVEMENT FORMULA AND CALCULATION**

$$\left( \frac{\text{Post-Group Total - Pre-Group Total}}{\text{Pre-Group Total}} \right) \times 100$$

$$\left( \frac{30 - 19}{19} \right) \times 100 \qquad \left( .5789 \right) \times 100 = 57.89\%$$

# 30-MiNUTE GROUPS

## CERTIFICATE
### OF COMPLETION

This Certificate is Presented to:

For Participating in the **Online Safety Group!**

Facilitator:

# ONLINE SAFETY GROUP
# COMPLETION LETTER

Date:_____

Hello!

Today was the final session in our Online Safety Group, and we wanted to let you know that your student has been presented with a Certificate of Completion.

Over the past ten sessions, we have reviewed the following topics:

- Technology Use

- Social Media: Pros and Cons

- Cybersecurity: Protecting Your Information

- Cybersecurity: Hacking, Phishing, and Scams

- Cybersecurity: Sextortion and Sexting

- Emotional Well-Being

- Being Kind Online

- Online Predators

- Artificial Intelligence

- Moving Forward

I am their counselor and will be available to them as needed. However, we will no longer be meeting every week. Please don't hesitate to contact me with any questions or concerns.

I am so proud of them and excited they were able to attend. Thank you so much for allowing them to participate in our Online Safety Group!

Warm regards,

_____

School Counselor

# Notes

1. Lohmann, R. C., & Smith, A. C. (2023). 15-Minute Focus: Digital Citizenship: Supporting Youth Navigating Technology in a Rapidly Changing World. National Center for Youth Issues.

2. Rothwell, J. (2023). How Parenting and Self-Control Mediate the Link Between Social Media Use and Youth Mental Health. Institute for Family Studies and The Gallup Organization, 11

3. CrowdStrike (2024). Annual Cybersecurity Report. https://www.crowdstrike.com/global-threat-report/

4. "Sextortion Awareness Video From San Jose Police Department | Office of Juvenile Justice and Delinquency Prevention," Office of Juvenile Justice and Delinquency Prevention, June 1, 2022. https://ojjdp.ojp.gov/media/video/32041

5. "Gavin's Law." South Carolina Department of Education. Accessed December 17, 2024. https://ed.sc.gov/newsroom/strategic-engagement/gavins-law/.

6. *The Daily Mail*, 1927 December 29, "Mail" Mustard and Cress, Quote Page 1, Column 8, Hull, Humberside, England.

7. Katella, K. (2024). How Social Media Affects Your Teen's Mental Health: A Parent's Guide. Yale Medicine.

8. Zhao, Y., Paulus, M. P., & Potenza, M. N. (2023). Brain structural co-development is associated with internalizing symptoms two years later in the ABCD cohort. Journal of Behavioral Addictions, 12(1), 80-93.

9. Vogels, Emily A. "Teens and Cyberbullying 2022." *Pew Research Center*, Pew Research Center, 15 Dec. 2022, www.pewresearch.org/internet/2022/12/15/teens-and-cyberbullying-2022/.

10. "Children and Grooming / Online Predators," Child Crime Prevention & Safety Center, n.d., https://childsafety.losangelescriminallawyer.pro/children-and-grooming-online-predators.html.

11. Finkelhor, D., Turner, H., & Colburn, D. (2022). Prevalence of online sexual offenses against children in the U.S. JAMA Network Open, 5(10), e2234471. https://doi.org/10.1001/jamanetworkopen.2022.34471

12. SentryPC, "Online Child Predator Statistics" SentryPC, n.d., https://www.sentrypc.com/home/statistics.htm#:~:text=We%20all%20know%20how%20wonderful,Crimes%20Against%20Children%20Research%20Center.

13. Lazic, Marija. "How Many Predators Are Online Each Day? [Online Predators Statistics]." May 19, 2023. https://legaljobs.io/blog/online-predators-statistics.

14. Internet crimes against children. Accessed December 17, 2024. https://ovc.ojp.gov/sites/g/files/xyckuh226/files/publications/bulletins/internet_2_2001/internet_2_01_6.html#:~:text=Only%20a%20fraction%20of%20all%20episodes%20was,exposure%20to%20sexual%20material%20told%20a%20parent.

15. "LibGuides: Digital Citizenship: Risky Online Relationships," n.d., https://ahs-asd103.libguides.com/c.php?g=413437&p=2817194.

16. Ibid

17. Lazic, Marija. "21 Alarming Online Predators Statistics." Legaljobs.io. LegalJobs. May 19, 2023. https://legaljobs.io/blog/online-predators-statistics#:~:text=Even%20though%20over%20half%20of

18. "Children and Grooming / Online Predators," Child Crime Prevention & Safety Center, n.d., https://childsafety.losangelescriminallawyer.pro/children-and-grooming-online-predators.html.

19. OpenAI. (2024). ChatGPT (June 20, 2024). OpenAI. Retrieved from https://www.openai.com/chatgpt

# ABOUT THE AUTHOR

**Raychelle Cassada Lohmann, Ph.D.**, is a counselor educator, clinical mental health counselor, school counselor, and international author of numerous books. Raychelle has expertise in a wide range of issues affecting children and adolescents, from anger and aggression to anxiety and depression to sexual trauma and bullying. Raychelle attended North Carolina State University, receiving her B.A. in psychology, her M.S. in counselor education, and her Ph.D. in counseling and counselor education. With 25 years in the counseling profession, Raychelle has devoted much of her time to working with children, adolescents, parents, and educators.

Raychelle is a licensed clinical mental health counselor supervisor and licensed school counselor in NC. She is also a licensed professional counselor in SC. Additionally, Raychelle is an EMDR-certified provider and holds the following certifications: Approved Clinical Supervisor (ACS), Board Certified Telemental Health Provider (BCTMH), Certified Clinical Trauma Professional (CCTP), and Global Career Development Facilitator (GCDF).

## A Brief Look at Raychelle's Workshop Sessions

### Big T and little t: Creating a Trauma-Sensitive School Environment

Nearly a quarter of the nation's youth will experience a traumatic event by age 16. Trauma can significantly impact young people's physical and mental health, affecting their ability to learn and excel academically. Therefore, schools are crucial in creating safe, supportive environments that foster resilience and promote healing. Whether it's a Big T event (i.e., unexpected loss of a loved one), little t occurrence (i.e., moving to a new school), or multiple complex traumas (i.e., exposure to pervasive abuse), the psychological effects can extend across a lifetime. Fortunately, there are essential coping skills that, if taught and nurtured, can significantly increase a youth's ability to heal and persevere. This interactive presentation aims to teach participants about Big T and little t events and explore trauma's neurological impact on young people. Furthermore, emphasis will be placed on building skills and implementing strategies to create a trauma-sensitive school environment where students do more than survive; they thrive.

### Digital Citizenship: Navigating Safely and Responsibly Online

In today's fast-paced, technology-driven world, our students are bombarded with massive amounts of information. Society's online transformation has paved previously unimaginable roadways of knowledge, adventure, and inspiration...as well as dangerous detours, hidden potholes, and hairpin turns. Educators must prepare their students with life skills to navigate safely and responsibly in a rapidly changing digital world. This interactive multi-media session aims to examine the benefits and drawbacks of technology and equip educators with practical skills and resources to guide their students in understanding what it means to be an upstanding digital citizen: one who is kind, responsible, and – most importantly – leaves an electronic footprint worthy of following.

### Disruptive Student Behavior: Addressing, Managing and Changing

Nationwide, schools are experiencing a rise in disruptive behaviors. Behavioral issues disturb the learning process, create peer conflict, interrupt the classroom, and lead to more staff exhaustion and faculty turnover. Educators know firsthand the time spent disciplining and redirecting unruly and challenging behaviors. The loss of instructional time addressing such behaviors affects the entire school community. Therefore, educators must have the knowledge and tools to prevent and manage these student behaviors. During this interactive multi-media session, participants will learn proactive and interventive strategies and engage in activities and case studies to deter challenging behaviors and promote positive ones. Participants will leave the session with practical and relevant tools and resources to address, manage and change disruptive behaviors, creating a peaceful conducive learning environment that bolsters student achievement.

### Exploring the Depths: Youth Anger, Aggression, and Rage

Anger is perhaps one of the most misunderstood emotions. It's the driving force that pushes us into action when we feel threatened, powerless, or mistreated. Anger can be both constructive and destructive, but unleashed through aggression, or rage can leave an aftermath of devastation. In schools, problematic anger can be met with hefty consequences such as being sent out of class to suspension or, worse, expulsion. Additionally, prolonged periods of anger have been linked with mental health issues such as anxiety, depression, substance use, and suicide. If you struggle with angry students, suit up because this engaging presentation will use a biopsychosocial lens to deeply understand the reasons, causes, and symptoms associated with anger. During the presentation, attendees will learn to gauge and monitor emotions and use evidence-based skills to help students decompress and manage their anger healthily and successfully.

### Gifting the Giver: Practicing Self-care and Preventing Burnout

Educators play a vital role in supporting students through complex challenges. Still, all too often, when giving to others, we neglect our emotional and physical well-being. This fun interactive, and empowering presentation will assist participants in putting first things first – themselves. Attendees will reflect on self-care practices and develop a personalized plan to nurture the nurturer. By the end of the presentation, participants will have a deeper understanding of the importance of self-care and be better equipped with practical tools to incorporate them into their professional and personal lives. When we care for ourselves, job satisfaction increases, burnout decreases, and we provide better student support. This presentation is a gift to the giver, the professional educators who freely give their time to promote wellness within their school community.

### Harnessing Superpowers: Helping Students Soar to Success

We all have superpowers. Powers that help us overcome unimaginable obstacles, get up when we get knocked down, and believe that our dreams are within our reach. We gain strength through three distinct energizing abilities: growth mindset, resilience, and grit. Although these three superpowers are related, each serves a distinct purpose in helping us soar to success. In this inspiring and empowering presentation, participants will engage in various interactive and creative activities and learn ways to help students discover and harness their internal superpowers. When students have a strong sense of self and believe in their ability to bounce back from adversity, they can maximize their potential making the impossible possible.

### Youth Mental Health Crisis: Strategies and Best Practices for School Professionals

Today more than ever, our young people are struggling with mental health issues. Youth mental health is cause for deep concern as rates of anxiety, attention-deficit/hyperactivity disorder, depression, self-harm, and suicide have been progressively increasing, creating a mental health crisis requiring urgent action. Schools play an instrumental role in answering the call for help by destigmatizing mental health issues, educating students, faculty, and parents, and serving as a liaison connecting students with much-needed mental health resources and support. This presentation will use a variety of interactive activities, group discussions, and case studies to examine the pressures and challenges faced by today's youth, including academic stress, social media influences, bullying, and societal expectations, as well as explore how the COVID-19 pandemic contributed to the crisis. Participants will leave the session with a deeper understanding of mental health risk factors, strategies, and best practices for identifying, supporting, and promoting student well-being.

**ncyionline.org/speakers**

---

# THE RESOURCES IN THIS BOOK ARE AVAILABLE FOR YOU AS A DIGITAL DOWNLOAD!

### Please visit **ncyi.org/30minonlinesafety** to access the downloadable resources.

### Enter the code below to unlock the resources:

## ONLINE566

NATIONAL CENTER for
**YOUTH ISSUES**

# About NCYI

National Center for Youth Issues provides educational resources, training, and support programs to foster the healthy social, emotional, and physical development of children and youth. Since our founding in 1981, NCYI has established a reputation as one of the country's leading providers of teaching materials and training for counseling and student-support professionals. NCYI helps meet the immediate needs of students throughout the nation by ensuring those who mentor them are well prepared to respond across the developmental spectrum.

## Connect With Us Online!

@nationalcenterforyouthissues

@ncyi

@nationalcenterforyouthissues